SOCIOCIDE AT THE 24/7

✻

SOCIOCIDE AT THE 24/7

✿

PAUL CUNNINGHAM

NEW MICHIGAN PRESS
TUCSON, ARIZONA

NEW MICHIGAN PRESS
DEPT OF ENGLISH, P. O. BOX 210067
UNIVERSITY OF ARIZONA
TUCSON, AZ 85721-0067

<http://newmichiganpress.com>

Orders and queries to <nmp@thediagram.com>.

Copyright © 2025 by Paul Cunningham. All rights reserved.

ISBN 978-1-934832-97-4. FIRST PRINTING.

Design by Ander Monson.

Cover image © Doberman84 | Dreamstime.com

CONTENTS

Sociocide at the 24/7   1

Acknowledgments   51

"I always thought I'd like my own tombstone to be blank. No epitaph, and no name. Well, actually, I'd like it to say 'figment.'"
— Andy Warhol, *America*

a queer tucked in by flowers
was it ashes or was it glitter

fingers of an era
flagged for farewell

satin-lined obscenity,
tulips crackling into ashes

was it ashes or was it glitter
at the end of nations?

(it was glitter)

WARNING: THIS PRODUCT
CONTAINS ADDICTIVE CHEMICALS

WARNING:
this big gulp delinquent's
gone 7/11 at the 24/7
gone all stations of the cross
at the Hollywood gas and go
BP Shell Sunoco
what i meant to say was
this is an insider's guide to
what to gas and how to die it
everything you wanted to know
about Prince Harry NOW
is this a convenient store or
IS THIS A CONVENIENT STORE???
members only members
are granted EARLY ACCESS
to exclusive content
CYBERTRUCKS, AM I RIGHT???
mmmmmmmmmm
Big Torn Campbell's Soup
Can YOU share
your most googled
fears? *I'm thinking*
the same

Fresh hot coffee ANY SIZE
don't burn me or I'LL SUE
another missing persons sign
conceals another bullethole
newsreels to channel
your inner Mad Men
your reaction to the reaction
is getting so many Likes
THIS IS EVERYTHING
WE KNOW SO FAR ABOUT
glass-clad polycarbonate
another attack on cashiers
on a different kind of screen
in the land of smash-and-grab
no safe transactions, only punch-ins
corruption and clock outs
measured by poolside fools
who only WANT IT ALL for
HALF THE PRICE

COLLECT THEM ALL:
science-backed rodent of voltaic spiral
ditto with the hypertension ditto what
the mirror flaunts ditto distorting
smudge of DNA the soft cursive pulse
of alphabet ditto with the numbers
traceless in the maze faceless if a protein
butchered by a name or another word
for accident
                    ditto like a hoax ditto
in the ripsnorting gray of this world
in the storm of it all in our carcass
country drunk on bloodlust dreams

EXPOSED SOFTWARE:
actually the gas and go
is nothing but a front
for a server farm
for data generative painting
a TMZ leak in real time
DUNH DUNH DUNH
creating new futures via
wish fulfillment via
deepfake laggers
fairy godmothers
gossip and rumors
it's an open source model
frequented by bad actors
i don't know
call it an immersive
art experience
i guess
if it sells
i mean
if it doesn't
Van Gogh
call it something
groundbreaking
compare it to
the Met Gala
et cetera
et cetera

something about
the art of
looking?

Mary's blackened skull speaks to me
as i order everything i can online
order everything i can
selfie with Mary Magdalene's FOOT BONE
selfie in Greece with her LEFT HAND
NOW let's do scientific facial reconstruction
and compare facial volume
MINE FOR YOURS, BABE
FIGMENT, it's one of those days, BABE
BABE i'm did this to myself
BABE i'm not even trying to sell anything
i don't think i like the people who watch us anymore
and since when did ME become an US?
fucking #gross
i don't think i like doing this anymore
even if i did get you through the pandemic
IT DOESN'T MATTER
#shoptherealdeal BABE
maybe i'm just your imagination
maybe i thought you thought I was doing something
REVOLUTIONARY
and maybe i think i don't think i am
but i'm reading years and years of birthday cards
from THE PAST that you and i share AND
WELL, i hate to say this, BUT
they all read: *i'm so proud of you*
CONGRATS!!!

ENCRYPTED

too much unseeable earth for
ailing geomancer, I
feeling out the cyber
bleeded out the hollows
of my hyssop veins
still feeling the scars
of a bitcoin haze
a coke-white darkness
glitching like an NFT candle
across shadowed bodies
what am i worth
a 4 eva 4 eva?

I RISE from this box
I RISE from any body's dreams
purple-winged, i ascend
IMAGINEER THAT
dizzy and choirless
outside the funeral home
like another flaking Godzilla
slowly baking in the sun
over and overdone
until nightfall
until the long beam
of a distant lighthouse
blue gestures in the sand
i want to be
cry freely
i want to be where the people are
as any monster in the feed
i'm sorry i meant to say
our FEED
polluted with flags
i meant *fags*
i refuse to let social media
police my language
police my feed
FAG FAG FAGGOTY FAGGOTRY
of fallen monuments
somewhere an unheard algorithm
and my pink spangled tears

           that
you hear me screaming
in the dance hall closet
scheming new ways
to warp your
dumb future

call me FIGMENT
call me, fatigued
storage for LOTS of photos
#getreadywithme
we need to leave this bed
but don't forget the props:
diamond pickaxe, diamond boots
STRONG enchantments
for SQUARE environments
haha #resign is trending every day

we need to leave this bed
that's what the BetterHelp twink says
do you get those YouTube ads
the BetterHelp twink knows what's best
paid actors pay no attention
these aren't the droids you're looking for
IN FACT pay no attention to THIS CALM
BEFORE THE STORM if you want
a reliable app to recalibrate your mind
Now downloading Paul Dano at the end of
L i t t l e   M i s s   S u n s h i n e
THEN YOU BETTER CRASH IT CRUSH IT
I SAY a walk through your local cemetery
is PERFECT for seeing your world open up
ESPECIALLY IF IT'S A LANDMARK CEMETERY
(sorry, i meant to say LANDLORD CEMETERY)
((a cemetery where they only bury landlords
lonely, loveless, fuckless, eyeless, soulless landlords))

Breakthrough lets you stay connected
to the people around you even when
collision on the east bound
Fire! Hot! Baja Blast, DO THAT SHIT
time to mine, time to contribute to society
(actually I'm only commenting to help
push further into the wrong algorithm)
actually my son broke his back on
one of those pull up bars, you know
the ones for rule-bending
CAN I GET A REFUND FOR
the inflammation and bruising
he's SO many colors now
you could call it hyperpigmentation
you could call it figment of your imagination
(you really have to experience it for yourself)

Who are you wearing
to the traffic jam? Primary colors again?
Amazon Essentials?
Wittgenstein's TRACTATUS?
with gold leaf dangling from the lips
and if THAT doesn't get me noticed
SHIT, that's it, I'll livetweet my next breakdown
mark my words mark ruffalo
to trend WATCH ME I'm being sincere
if I don't get some Snoop Dogg ASMR ASAP
i don't know about you, but i'm totally ready
to learn something new and
NOW with tomorrow's forecast...

Mary, Mary quite contrary
displayed in a golden reliquary
How does your garden grow?
i think i   figured out most things
about life   when i was 5 years old
watching   the office scene
at the end   of *Willy Wonka*
half a sink   half a vault
half a clock   half a self
some people   only get to live life
 in halves   especially children
some have   only half until 14
 some have   only half until 21
some have   only half into their 30s
   have of   themselves, you see
   have of   themselves
can you   see Charlie's mascara
running   lipstick on his teeth
   alone   he's much older now
et cetera   *et cetera*
kneeling   alone inside a long ago
  Wonka   vator shattered roof
like some   stained glass scene
et cetera   *et cetera*
   wrong sir   wrong
     it's all   a scar
       a growth   a grown up
        can't you   see Charlie
          trying   to be
            something
           he's not
             never
              was

yo what is up guys
today i am doing my best
to exploit tragedies
for increased revenue

by becoming a patron
you can help me become
a force for good TBH
i have big hopes

by becoming a patron
you can add payment details
which won't just help me
but will help build my brand

finally, i don't know
who needs to hear this
but i love the way
you growth today

world wide
garden of cruelty
haywire darkness on laburnum trails
where the hackers root up onion
where the children all go
missing
golden, oublietted
into virtual chains

YOU'RE ON FACEBOOK LIKE AN AD
bescreened with hidden IP
doesn't matter, like-mind
in the deep, dark game
shareholding holo shares
they call this gyre augmentation
shoot it up like roidy baddies
never erring on TV
trails of crime, a social stream
don't ever find yourself offscreen
don't get caught, don't be mistaken
for computer fraud
don't be shaken for not sharing
it's the caring we connect to
call it your environment
sharing every share
social environment
let's call it social for short
ecstasy for sure
let's call it niche for like-minds
let's call the "let's" me
now let me take your time
so many vacancies
for big data bodies on the social
they contract real nice
they transact real gneiss
down the craggy adware column
bidding like an auction series

encrypting in the dark it tastes like
onion peel, it tastes hyperreal
currency is virtual
like all you onion kids
in the system-breach
leaky email box
of the hacking team
where the onions grow
all suspiciously
so suspiciously

SO a designer to watch is
slashing seasons ahead
as a magazine asks me
when I last felt timeless
and it might be this poem
in which I am reacting
to future reactions
influenced by the
present-day trend
of being that which
has yet to be determined

(in other words
the anticipation is
killing me)

CHOOSE YOUR PREFERRED EXPERIENCE
pulse-pounding PUNCH UP THE SOUND
PLEASE thought-provoking
I'M TRYING TO GIVE A TED-TALK
time-stopping PUNCH IT UP
LIKE A PUNCH TO THE STOMACH
LIKE A BLURB BY A SCAR
LIKE A KICK TO THE FACE
LIKE A LIE, LIKE A LIE
piece by piece, latest exercise
branded like a generator
PLEASE CUE DISGUISE
SWITCH IT ON NOW
IN YOUR FACES
REVOLUTION

LOOK AT ME: i'm fat with relics
slow-dancing with a bag of Takis
my therapist says: *become the person*
you're afraid of becoming
but subscribers tell me:
you're going to an early grave
CHOO CHOO, buy my merch, I guess
before I lose it all in crypto
in a hospital gown (#ass)
too weak to use my own inhaler
i thought I was striations in ONE DIRECTION
amino acids of all life on earth recorded
i just wish i could feel luminous again
maybe i can sell my iPhone's gold
0.034 grams of gold
0.34 grams of silver
0.015 grams of palladium
(THE HELL IS PALLADIUM?)
mommy and daddy told me:
One day you'll sell out stadiums!
my iPhone's gold average?
two dollars fifty cents
I'm unsure you'll ever read this
so time to post another selfie
but I think you're doing a good job
how time of you
time to perform for my fans
as i go unnoticed ordering

three orders of Denny's Grand Slam
YOU CALLED IT: breakfast for dinner
who doesn't love to pretend an ending
is always another beginning...
the very beginning...
like an alphabet or something...
honestly, I'm very healthy...
CHOO CHOO, buy my merch
LIKE AND SUBSCRIBE

i have trouble using the internet
to PORTION CONTROL
i try not to eat anything found in a search engine
i try to save energy and prioritize
EASY CLEANUP
but if i order NOW
three dishwasher-free easy payments
will turn into a 30-day money back guarantee
and as the phone's wound begins to grow, i realize
i've never been promised such a world

America is
what changes
every minute
with limp trap
eze management
and maternitywear
to-die-for poli
cies at a fraction
of the price O!
Virgin Pulse
sweet biometric data
Did you get your
steps in today? asks the administrative hardware
employed by the overworked
and under-responding administrative team
Did I ever! written by torso-sourcers
those get-rich-quick incels
Who can't get enough business retreats
masquerading as healers
rattlers quick to slurp
whatever life's left
for the scraping
HOW'S THAT FOR WELLNESS
from the floor of the gas and go
a big league chewing
such big, big boys
with no real grip
nothing to fill the cracks

in their concrete tummies
only repeat ICEE spills
across the buttery floortile
of a RealD 3D experience
exposing ol' country homes
half-assed by landlords
hungry for new leases
and chalk outlines
YEE-HAW

Are YOU struggling to STAY ALIVE?
well my BULLSHIT only takes SECONDS
and by seconds i mean that
THIS takes MINUTES
THIS takes just FIVE MINUTES
ON YOUR FLOOR FOR ONLY TEN MINUTES
THAT'S ALL IT TAKES JUST ONE HOUR
now let's loosen up that lumbar spine
HEY what's that sound from your lungs?
are you feeling challenged by
your resting energy expenditure?
WELL i'm going to tell you why that is
i'm going to toss you
into a mirror SO HARD
you'll feel broken
i'm going to shatter your face
and i'm going to prepare you for
FULL BODY BURN
UNTIL YOU CAN'T BREATHE
UNTIL YOU CAN'T STAND
without worry
EAT! EAT! EAT!
just eat JUST FUCKING EAT
if you don't, how will you expend?
HIT THAT SNOOZE BUTTON AGAIN
order pizza from your BED
burn calories in BED (for real BRO)
salad is for weakling FAGS

not for VSHRED DADDIES in the know
what you need to know is ME
and where you're wanting to go
TAKE MY FREE METABOLIC QUIZ
and leave your friends and families
S P E E C H L E S S
NOW click to play CLICK THE LINK
answer the questions and get
REAL RESULTS   REAL RESULTS
REAL RESULTS

xQc FOR MAYOR
doesn't it feel good to feel understood
NOW let me level up during this
housing shortage
(almost read HOUSING as HOSTAGE)
I GOTTA GET OUT OF THIS NEIGHBORHOOD
all the green space is full, I mean
all the green space is TRUE
YOUR FAULT SUCK IT UP
FIND A JOB
NOPE, you just died of
BLACK LUNG
you just died of
DYSENTERY
can't ford a river
can't caulk a wagon
WHAT IS YOUR CHOICE?
WHAT IS FREE WILL?
you guys, guess what
me and my girlfriend finally did the thing
and can't afford to finish
(BLOCKED FROM CHAT)

my apartment collapsed tonight
please visit the link to my kickstarter
my teacher is a dumbass
and she can't even afford to buy
her own dry erase markers
and that's why i need you to donate
to MY kickstarter because
i happen to be depressed
then again you might not give a fuck
about any of that
but my teacher, like, can't even dry erase
because she has no markers that do that
though, more important things are happening
(i guess)
Drake is telling his girl drama
the air pollution has given us
cardiovascular disease
all hail our supreme leader
finally we do something besides
gambling and watching tiktok
the traffic now knows
where to go and
where not to go
and somehow [LOOK]
you are
[HERE]

i don't know where the fudge i am
some dumbass professor at this college i hate
talking about Baudrillard at 8am
even if i'm wake n bake
in my Family Guy pajama pants
even if all money IS worth less over time
yet you recommend i evacuate
because another school shooter
is hungry for skulls?
well they can have my skull
they can have it
IMMEDIATELY
NOW MOVE CAM TOP RIGHT
NOW MOVE CAM BOTTOM LEFT
now DAISY now PLUTO
now DONALD now GOOFY
In your fantasy, am I duck or dog?
i can't even distinguish
your hand from mine
i can't even OnlyFans
because only bullets trend [HERE]
relatively high
i'm feeling pretty high
for a fluctuating price
precious metals BABE
i feel like that time i was a kid
and got lost in Epcot
where everything looks like everything
only somehow worse

Is your hand even still there?
actually, there is no sensation anymore
Mickey, i think it's working
i feel so numb now so
do whatever you
want to me

my what large accounts you have
ALL THE BETTER TO SEE YOU WITH
my dear oh dear overheard in a report to HIM
classified glassified body technology
cloaked for the scraping the taking NOW KNEEL
THERE ARE NO AD-FREE ZONES
now don't get things twisted
you are valued you are
a TRUE SUBJECT
anyway that's how it reads
in the search results

how do i
how do i see the metadata of an image
how do i search
how do i search for a dot
how do i search for a word in a google doc
search for a song an image
search for a person
how do i search for a person
how do i search for a person
how do i search for a person
a person is
a person is septic
a person is
a person is free
a person is free from
what does free from mean
a person is flying a kite on a beach
a person is killed in a collision every
a person is every
every time or everytime
a person is a search
every time or everytime
a person is a search for
a person is a search for a song an image
a person is a search for a person
a song an image
add a song to an image
how do i

how do i add a song to an image
how do i add a song to an image

APPLE VISION PRO you really have to
experience it for yourself
everyone who is pro-cruise ships deserves this
Poor skull, thy fingers set ablaze
Call it an investment, call me FIGMENT
Next stop: IMAGINATION
in a time of endless violence
rose-crowned and diamond-eyed my crypto skull
carries a magic 8 BALL by mouth
i promise to swallow every question you have
In me behold the only skull
your eyes? . . . literally me
Next stop: "Sail Away" by Enya

DAMN IT Bobby
we are de-evolving as a species
we are the kind of thing you find on INSTAGRAM
when you SCROLL for too long
we sound like a public restroom
someone make this a song please
i actually really love the sound cardinals make
BRO my pet cardinal is literally
the sound of my childhood
one time i played the sounds a mockingbird makes
for my undergrads and they were like
THIS SONG SLAPS—*are you sure this isn't AI?*
I MEAN imagine setting up a camera
in that many rooms of your house…

you know the economy is usually bad when
the content just keeps getting funnier

imagine telling your principal
you want whatever BRO is on
BRO has some of the tippiest toes
BRO i'm from Florida we go up to gators all the time
like little dogs some will fuck with you
some won't that's life
BRO what the fuck
BRO just leveled up
BRO is ripped today and works as a model
BRO never passes the blunt in rotation
BRO deserves an oscar
BRO been waiting all day to drink non-alcoholic sparkling water
BRO po that bubbly
BRO ain't even with us anymore
BRO my dad is humming the X-files theme
BRO your dad knows how to hit those notes
i want whatever BRO is on

I DON'T KNOW
is this all supposed to be
some kind of CELEBRITY PORTRAIT?
a voice versus a perfect voice
for serious legendary status
WAYYYY better than the recording
not just an icon but a great mom
and yes, i remembered your birthday
but you don't know me
GOOD LORD she's ICONIC
the collab no one asked for but
somehow always needed
I BEG TO DIFFER
this ain't country, country ain't about nudity
but SHUT UP she is so dope I CAN'T stop watching
this really long ADIDAS advertisement
BRO i almost broke the mouse hitting LIKE
i mean she IS from Texas
i love looking at her looking at herself in the mirror
31 songs is I CAN'T SLEEP
please appreciate Posty's background vocals
BE blessed and BE a blessing
HIS tattoos appear on HER face DUMBASS
i don't know who needs to hear this
but we are all in this together
just mesmerized by her total self-acceptance
they will forever be a legend
Why are you acting like you

don't know this song?
no flashy gimmicks
she IS the MOMENT a bundle of JOY
under fire for brusque behavior
media buncha liars she was polite
ASK A QUESTION GET AN ANSWER
she looked stunnin' what do y'all want
why is he walking around with a sock on his face
Some people are saying you're controlling
would you like to respond to your haters?
I'm a person BRO, you got kids
ALL OF THIS TMZ BULLSHIT I DON'T GIVE A
FUCK
you think because you're a white woman you
can ask about my wife's free will?
I'M A LEGEND
DUDE, he offered her a job at the end LOL
DUDE is out of his trash mind
he's a villain not a legend
AS IT WAS?
more like: IT IS
WHAT IT IS
every morning i wake up scary
Hairy, i smile thinking of you
when this song first came out I was homeless,
on drugs, and then jail NOW
i have a house, job, and husband
am *I* so annoyingly catchy

i wanna go back in time so bad
Did you know that
as we grow up
everything changes?
How many glasses do YOU wanna break?
Adele: YES
WHO'S HERE IN 2024???
WHO'S HERE IN 2025???
WHO'S HERE IN 2026???
we just time traveled, YOU FEEL ME?
i can't believe this song has aged like this
WELL, she can sing and she is BEAUTIFUL
LEAVE HIM ALONE
he's here to have fun
good for her   LET HER FANS RAGE
working out 3 times a day doesn't fit
into most people's lifestyles
but GOOD FOR HER
can someone tell me the title of this song?
"Bitch looks too fat"
"Bitch looks too skinny"
haters are going to hate
no matter what you do
i can't   ENOUGH
body image tore shit down
i appreciate you being so vocal
about body image i dream
i dream of the way she said "Hi Mom"

and "Oh that's my Dad"
old Hollywood glamour DOES IT AGAIN
Does Oscar de la Renta want
to make YOU a dress?
she is dropped jaw and
modern-day Marilyn Monroe
CAN'T STOP HIM
red backless suit is too feminine
too cringe, so disgusting
what TF happened to American men
more like Timothy Shambles
i think he is gorgeous and stunning
he is the man who fell to earth
i don't love when he wears
feminine clothes tho
idk tho they look sincerely happy
hella soothing voices
i used to HATE this HER but
now i'm like good job sport what's good
i think his voice needs therapy
"Peaches" will be sung at my funeral
but i want it to be sung by Jack Black himself
intro gives me chills like how
it felt to open a Polly Pocket playset
for the first time no wonder
no wonder she was cast
she's perfect she's flawless
he's so lovely he's so down to earth

she's so beautiful i'm crying
into my echo mic under a lilac bush
in some reese's pieces backyard
in some forgotten 90s

i don't know what to say
there's no heavy perfume behind me
NOW only the original garment
NOW i wear my enthusiasm
on my blouson sleeve
there's no arguing with me:
fashion IS sound
a S C R O O P of fabric
catwalk extravaganzas
a force field of lab-grown diamond
infinite bangle
effortless style meets weightless protection
a S C R O O P of glitter
the original garment is haute couture tour de force
not non-gendered but identity expansive
no need to tie up any loose ends
i'm decidedly decadent
and taking charge
call it a new direction
BOURGEOIS from the front
BANG from the side

for the love of garments
i am GUILTY
charged with and convicted of
allegedly obstructing officers
arrested on suspicion of driving under
the influence and ordered to pay
for the release of photographs
during a club appearance

POETRY remains a signature experience
WELL WORN a merry melange
of patterns and textures
the FEED of your GOOGLE SEARCH

rules forever bending unto a
mi casa su casa ethos
& must-have styling essentials
i.e. THE LATEST
la vie est belle

ACKNOWLEDGMENTS

My utmost gratitude to Ander Monson for taking a chance on this little book of noisy voices and zany optics. Grateful thanks also goes to Joyelle McSweeney, Jonathan Crary, and Ben Fama for their generous engagement with *Sociocide at the 24/7*.

PAUL CUNNINGHAM co-manages Action Books. He is the author of two poetry collections from Schism Press: *Fall Garment* (2022) and *The House of the Tree of Sores* (2020). He is one of the collaborators featured in Katrine Øgaard Jensen's *Ancient Algorithms* (Sarabande Books, 2025). His writing has appeared in venues like *DIAGRAM*, *Denver Quarterly*, *BOMB Magazine*, *The Texas Review*, *Bat City Review*, *Quarterly West*, and many others. Cunningham is a coordinator of the International Network for Comparative Studies and sits on the board of NonfictioNOW. He currently manages the MFA in Creative Writing Program at the University of Notre Dame where he also teaches.

❈

COLOPHON

Text is set in a digital version of Jenson, designed by Robert Slimbach in 1996, and based on the work of punchcutter, printer, and publisher Nicolas Jenson. The titles here are in Futura, which is the best font for titles.